APRIL KIHLSTROM'S BOOK IN A WEEK WORKBOOK

BY

APRIL KIHLSTROM

© Copyright 2013 April Kihlstrom

All rights reserved. No part of this book may be reproduced in any form without the express written permission from the copyright holder except in the case of brief quotations for professional articles or reviews.

"I have just completed my second BIAW with April. There are few other writing courses I've done that can hold a candle to April's. (Okay, there are two others, and they were technical ones pertaining to crime scene investigations).

April doesn't just take you through BIAW. She nurtures you and answers every single query. Best of all, she makes writers ask themselves questions which broaden the scope of their work. Information such as 'Pay attention to how fears affect your speech patterns' is what sets April's tutorials apart from others. She also doesn't just ask you who your target audience is, but tutors you to write according to those readers.

Many BIAW courses preach the old standard 'silence the inner critic and just write' or 'why do you want to write this book?' But April goes deeper. She doesn't just want you to post the numbers of words you achieved each day; she wants to hold you accountable and create a group dynamic.

I personally relate to April's system of creating a character chart, something I find one of the best writing tools ever as it can be referred to throughout the writing of the book, and also if I'm writing a series.

And something that is the crux of these BIAW tutorials? April prepares you for the actual writing days, so that you are ready to go and don't have to worry about your inner critic because you are so keen to get those words down by that stage. And that is what it's all about." --Vonnie Hughes, published author

DEDICATION

This workbook is dedicated to all the wonderful writers who have taken my online Book in a Week class or attended my workshops. This workbook would not exist or be what it is without their enthusiasm, their support and the wonderful questions they have asked me. To all of them I say: Thank you from the bottom of my heart!

INTRODUCTION

This workbook is intended to help writers plan out their books in a way that is organic. Most of us write linearly but brainstorm in a nonlinear way. If one thinks of writing a book as being similar to putting together a puzzle, this workbook is intended to help writers create some of the key puzzle pieces.

You don't need to answer the questions in order; in fact I strongly recommend jumping around and first answering those where answers come easily. Read the questions and give your subconscious a chance to figure out answers to the rest. Some answers you may never know or need on a conscious level. Other answers may give you ideas for plot or information to include in your book.

Experience has taught me that both the value and the success of a Book in a Week challenge often depend directly on the brainstorming an author has done beforehand. This workbook is intended also to help prepare you if you are considering trying Book in a Week.

Note: This workbook cannot fully replace my online Book in a Week class but it will give you a sense of some of what I cover in that class. For more information on Book in a Week, please see my website www.aprilkihlstrom.com or take my online Book in a Week class.

I have separated the workbook into fiction and nonfiction and many of the questions overlap--because that's the nature of writing. My hope is that it will be less confusing and easier to find what applies to YOUR writing by having this division in the workbook.

All of the material in this book comes from my experience as a multi-published author and teaching both fiction and nonfiction writers in my online Book in a Week writing class. I hope you will find this material as useful as the students in my classes have.

Note: I often suggest that authors use index cards--one per person or character and one per scene or section of a chapter. They are easy to carry, encourage the use of key words rather than sentences or paragraphs and can be shuffled around to create a kind of outline. They are particularly handy when characters or people or events carry over into other books.

TABLE OF CONTENTS

APRIL KIHLSTROM'S BOOK IN A WEEK WORKBOOK 1
DEDICATION 3
INTRODUCTION 3
FICTION 6
    WHY ARE YOU WRITING THIS? 6
    WHO IS IN YOUR BOOK? 7
    WHAT HAPPENS IN YOUR BOOK? FOR EACH SCENE ASK: 15
    STRUCTURE 17
    SENSORY DETAILS 19
    DETAILS USEFUL TO SHOW NOT TELL: 23
    DIALOGUE 24
    BRAINSTORMING EXERCISES--FOR ANY NOVEL: 26
    BRAINSTORMING EXERCISES--FOR LITERARY FICTION: 28
    BRAINSTORMING EXERCISES--FOR SCIENCE FICTION: 29
    BRAINSTORMING EXERCISES--FOR ROMANCE: 31
    BRAINSTORMING EXERCISES--FOR MURDER/MYSTERY: 34
    BRAINSTORMING EXERCISES--FOR HORROR: 36
NONFICTION 37
    WHY ARE YOU WRITING THIS? 37
    WHO IS IN YOUR BOOK? 38
    WHAT HAPPENS IN YOUR BOOK OR WHAT POINTS DO YOU WANT TO MAKE? 47
    DECIDING ON A STRUCTURE FOR YOUR BOOK: 49
    SENSORY DETAILS: 50
    DETAILS USEFUL TO SHOW NOT TELL: 54
    BRAINSTORMING EXERCISES--FOR NONFICTION: 55
MEMOIRS 57
    BASIC MEMOIRS—IF YOU DON'T KNOW WHERE TO BEGIN 57
    SPECIFIC EXPERIENCE THAT MATTERS TO YOU 60
    MORE MEMOIR BRAINSTORMING QUESTIONS 63
PREPARATION FOR BOOK IN A WEEK 66
    REAL LIFE PREPARATION: 66
    MENTAL/EMOTIONAL PREPARATION: 66
    WRITING PREPARATION: 67

BOOK IN A WEEK 68
ACTUAL WRITING WEEK 68
EACH DAY AS YOU BEGIN TO WRITE 69
IF YOU GET STUCK 70
AT THE END OF EACH DAY 70

EVALUATING THE BOOK IN A WEEK EXPERIENCE 71
PRACTICAL MATTERS 71
HOW YOU WRITE 73
WHO YOU ARE AS A WRITER--FICTION? 74
WHO YOU ARE AS A WRITER--NONFICTION? 74
WHO YOU ARE AS A WRITER--BOTH FICTION AND NONFICTION? 75

AUTHOR'S NOTE 77
PICTURES 78
NOTES 81
CHARACTER LIST 90

FICTION

Why are you writing this?

1) What matters to YOU about this story or material? Why do you want to write it? Another way to phrase this is: What do you love and/or care most about the book you want to write?

2) Who are you writing this for? Who is your target audience? (The more specific you are, the easier it will be to figure out the most effective way to write your book.) Why this group? What are they looking for in the kind of book you're writing?

3) What do you want readers to remember long after they read this book? How do you want them to FEEL?

4) What is the style/tone/approach most likely to appeal to your target audience? (Examples: mystery, romance, humor, drama, scholarly, folksy, etc. More than one adjective may apply.)

Who is in your book?

1) Name, age, description

2) WHY this person is important to your book?

3) What impact does this person have on others?

4) What is most unique about this person?

5) Family

6) Things the person does—either work or interests, hobbies or...whatever YOU choose

7) Types of things the person says, thinks, wishes, dreams, hopes, does

8) How will this person change or grow?

9) How will his/her situation change?

10) What beliefs or stories do your characters have or tell themselves--about life, the world, other people and themselves?

11) Which beliefs will be challenged over the course of the book?

12) Which stories will change and how will they change? Which beliefs will each character end up keeping?

13) How does each character react to having his or her stories or beliefs challenged?

14) Who is supportive and who isn't?

15) What does each character gain by changing the stories they tell themselves?

16) What is the person's personal code of honor (even for villains!)? WHY is this his/her code?

17) What is/was the person's deepest fear? Why—where did it come from?

18) What does/did the person secretly dream of accomplishing/having? Why?

19) What are this person's rituals and/or traditions? (Note: Rituals and traditions can be religious or something as simple as what they eat every day for breakfast or wear when they watch their favorite sports team or how they celebrate a holiday or birthday or what they do right before they do _____.)

20) What is/was the person's greatest flaw?

21) What do you love/like/admire about the person?

22) What kinds of people will readers expect to see in your type of book?

23) What kinds of people do you want to write about?

24) How would this person's friends describe him or her?

25) How would an enemy describe this person?

26) What is unexpected about the person?

27) HOW IS THIS PERSON LIKE THE PEOPLE WHO WILL BE READING YOUR BOOK—or perhaps like someone they know?

28) How did or do the people you're writing about feel about change in general? What about a particular change?

29) What action(s) might they take as a result of this change?

30) What got or will get better because of the change? What did or will get worse because of it?

31) How might or did the person change/grow/learn? What kinds of events could/would cause this to happen?

32) What would this person change if he/she could? How does he or she try to do so?

33) What does the person hate doing? What circumstances might cause the person to have to do it?

34) What would it be handy for your person to do but he or she can't? Who might he or she have to depend on for help and under what circumstances? OR How might they learn to do it?

35) What does your person love to do? How can you use that?

36) What does the person choose to wear and why? Who doesn't like it and what happens when he/she dresses that way anyway?

37) How does you're the person feel about family? Who does he/she fight with? Who is loving?

38) Is the person a conformist or a rebel? Is that going to change during the course of the book and if so how and as a result of what events?

39) What has the person never told anyone? (In a romance, having your hero or heroine tell the other this secret will signal an immense step forward in intimacy.)

40) What rituals, if any change—and how can you use these changes to show the reader the person has changed? Or is it the reader, if you're writing nonfiction, who you want to change one or more rituals (such as watching TV every evening instead of exercising or working on a project)?

41) Are the rituals and traditions one person wants to follow in conflict with the rituals and traditions someone else wants to follow. (Note: This is often a challenge newlywed couples face if the respective families have very different holiday or birthday traditions. OR sometimes one person in a family wants to change traditions/rituals and others don't.)

42) What else is important about your characters?

What happens in your book? For each scene ask:

1) Where and when does this event or scene happen?

2) What causes the event?

3) Who is involved?

4) WHAT CHANGES AS A RESULT OF THIS SCENE OR EVENT? (Who changes/grows or could change or grow? How? And how does this inevitably lead to later events?) Another way to look at this is to ask: How does someone's story change or begin to change as a result of this scene or event?

5) Any other details you can think of about the event.

6) What is at stake? You want to ask this question for each major character in the scene.

7) How will this scene impact each major character EMOTIONALLY and cause him or her to question and perhaps begin to rewrite some story about his/her life?

8) Why is this scene important to the overall novel? If I took it out would the story still be as compelling? (If so, take it out. If not, look to see how you can make it even more compelling.)

9) How does this scene naturally grow out of the actions and reactions that have already taken place in the book?

10) If you filmed this scene, what would the characters be DOING that reflects their internal emotional state? (In other words, you're looking for ways to show the contrast between internal feelings and external words OR to show that they match. Your tools are: speech patterns, facial expressions, body language, words spoken, and actions taken.)

Structure

1) What changes for your character(s) at the beginning of the book?

2) How will the characters handle the change? What happens as a result of that?

3) What events MUST happen in this book?

4) Why will your characters find themselves involved in such events?

5) How will each event be caused by previous events (due to reactions and thus actions of one or more characters)?

6) How might you keep increasing the stakes and what will provide counterpoint moments to intense emotion—a chance to figuratively and perhaps literally a chance to catch one's breath?

7) What might your "black moment" be?

8) What do your characters gain by the end of the story?

Sensory details:*(Note: Include how your characters FEEL about each of these things. Some may be neutral Most have probably never stopped to think about them but...perhaps one or more has. PLAY with possibilities.)*

1) What is the setting? Rural? Urban? Suburban? Alien/foreign? Be as specific as you can—not by the name of the locale but its characteristics.

2) What kinds of buildings are there? What are they made out of? What kind of comforts do or don't they have?

3) What kinds of stores exist? What are they like? What is the process of shopping like for the people in YOUR book? What stores do which people notice and use? What do people in your book make for themselves instead of buying?

4) What kind of transportation exists? What does it look, sound, and perhaps smell like? What are the good things and what are the challenges with that kind of transportation?

5) What do people eat and drink? How does it taste and smell? Do people use utensils (what kind?) or eat with their hands? What's a luxury? What's common, every day?

6) What occupations and diversions exist? (How do people dress for those things? Where do they do them?)

7) What kind of plumbing and trash disposal exists?

8) What is the weather like?

9) What is the landscape like?

10) How do key characters or people in your book:

Look

Dress

Move

Sound

Smell

11) How do key objects (which may include rooms in a house):

Look

Taste

Feel

Smell

Sound

Details useful to show not tell:

For each major character:

1) List 5 things that scare him or her.

2) List 5 things that make him or her feel safe

3) List 5 physical reactions he or she has when scared

4) List 5 things he or she does when unsure of himself or herself

5) List 5 things he or she does when feeling safe and/or happy

Dialogue

1) Who will be speaking? Why these people?

2) What will the dialogue tell readers about these people that they do not already know?

3) Why and/or how is this dialogue important to the plot?

4) What ISN'T being said that's important? Is there a difference between what the person is actually thinking and feeling and what he/she is saying? How can you signal these things to the reader?

5) For each speaker, what is the person's natural style of speaking? What kinds of words would he or she naturally choose? What kind of sentence structure? How does this pattern change under pressure or intense emotion?

6) What body language and/or facial expressions might accompany what's being said? (If you were reading this aloud or acting it out in a play, what would you do to convey the emotions and indicate what perhaps isn't being said?) How can you weave this information along with the actual dialogue?

Brainstorming Exercises--for any novel:

1) What kind of book do your readers want to read?

2) What do YOUR readers care about?

3) What is your character's personal code of honor?

4) What does your character want to achieve? What—or who—will stand in his or her way?

5) What is the character's deepest fear?

6) How does a relationship with other characters embody that deepest fear in some way-- or require facing that fear?

7) What is the character's secret dream--which he or she has never shared with anyone? What might cause him/her to share it with another character?

8) What does the character usually say or do when upset? Scared? Happy? Confident? (I'm talking mannerisms, speech patterns, activities.)

9) What is the character's greatest strength?

10) What is the character's greatest flaw?

11) How would a friend describe this character?

12) How would an enemy describe this character?

Brainstorming Exercises--for Literary Fiction:

1) What is your theme?

2) Who is/are your primary character(s)?

3) Does your primary character change and grow? Why or why not?

4) What are your character's fears?

5) What are your character's goals?

6) What stands in the way of your character's goals?

7) What "slice of life" are you trying to show?

Brainstorming Exercises--for Science Fiction:

1) What is your world structure?

2) What is/are the culture(s) you will be using for the characters in your book?

3) What is the political structure of the society in your book?

4) Do you have aliens? If so, how do they interact with humans or do they do so at all? Are there any humans in your story?

5) What is your primary theme?

6) What does your protagonist learn and/or accomplish?

7) What is your protagonist's main goal?

8) What are the obstacles your protagonist faces in reaching his/her goal?

9) Who helps your protagonist reach this goal?

10) Who interferes with your protagonist reaching this goal?

11) How will your protagonist overcome inner and outer obstacles? Or will he/she fail to do so?

Brainstorming Exercises--for Romance:

1) Picture hero/heroine in a fight--what would it be over? Why?

2) Loving--what would touch the heroine's heart? The hero's heart?

3) What would make your characters cry?

4) What would make your characters work together--no matter how angry they are at each other?

5) What could make them rise above their fears to do what must be done?

6) What is the hero's deepest secret and how will the heroine find out? What is hers and how will he find out?

7) What would the hero consider unforgivable? How about the heroine?

8) What are their highest values and deepest needs?

9) How will each main character grow? How will the other main character help this character grow?

10) In what ways can and will the hero make the heroine--and any woman--feel safe?

11) In what ways can the heroine help the hero feel safe enough to face HIS fears?

12) What do the hero and heroine discover about love that they didn't know before?

13) How are they stronger/better/wiser/safer/happier together than they ever could be alone?

Brainstorming Exercises--for Murder/Mystery:

1) Who dies and how? Or, if not a murder, WHAT is the focus of the mystery?

2) How is the body found? Or, what is found? How? Why? By whom? Under what circumstances?

3) What clues will you need to plant and who will find/notice them? Your detective? The reader?

4) Scenes of interrogation. Who asks the questions? Who answers--and why or why not?

5) Scenes of confrontation. Who fights? Why? What motive will this give the person(s)? Who, if anyone, overhears the confrontation?

6) What will surprise the reader—or the person solving the crime?

7) What are the hopes and dreams and fears of the person solving the mystery?

8) What are the killer's hopes? Dreams? Fears? Justification for what he/she does?

Brainstorming Exercises--for Horror:

1) What is the focus of the horror and how is it revealed?

2) Who discovers the horror? When? How?

3) What is the hero/heroine's greatest fear and how does it tie into the horror?

4) How does the hero/heroine overcome this fear? (What incident allows the character to rise above the fear?)

5) If more than one character will resolve the dilemma of the horror, what happens so that the characters realize they must work together?

6) What conflicts might tear the group apart—and how are they revealed?

NONFICTION

Why are you writing this?

1) What matters to YOU about this story or material? Why do you want to write it? Another way to phrase this is: What do you love and/or care most about the book you want to write?

2) Who are you writing this for? Who is your target audience or...who is it important to you and/or would it make you HAPPY to write for? (The more specific you are, the easier it will be to figure out the most effective way to write your book.) Why this group? What are they looking for in the kind of book you're writing?

3) What do you want readers to remember long after they read this book? How do you want them to FEEL?

4) What is the style/tone/approach most likely to appeal to your target audience? (Examples: mystery, romance, humor, drama, scholarly, folksy, etc. More than one adjective may apply.)

Who is in your book?

Note: Not all questions will apply in nonfiction but because nonfiction can span such a variety of works, I am including all of these. Choose those relevant to YOUR book and ignore the rest.

1) Name, age, description

2) WHY this person is important to your book?

3) What impact did this person have on others?

4) What is most unique about this person?

5) Family

6) Things the person does—either work or interests, hobbies or...whatever YOU choose

7) Types of things the person says, thinks, wishes, dreams, hopes, does

8) How did this person change or grow?

9) How did his/her situation change?

10) How is this person's story relevant to the points you want to make? What anecdote(s) do you want to share?

11) What stories or beliefs do the people in your book have or tell themselves--about life, the world, other people and themselves?

12) Which beliefs will be challenged over the course of the book?

13) Which stories will change and how will they change? Which beliefs will each person end up keeping?

14) How does each person react to having his or her stories or beliefs challenged?

15) What does each person gain by changing the stories they tell themselves?

16) What is the person's personal code of honor (even for villains!)? WHY is this his/her code?

17) What is/was the person's deepest fear? Why—where did it come from?

18) What does/did the person secretly dream of accomplishing/having? Why?

19) What are this person's rituals and/or traditions? (Note: Rituals and traditions can be religious or something as simple as what they eat every day for breakfast or wear when they watch their favorite sports team or how they celebrate a holiday or birthday or what they do right before they do _____.)

20) What is/was the person's greatest flaw?

21) What do you love/like/admire about the person?

22) What kinds of people will readers expect to see in your type of book?

23) What kinds of people do you want to write about?

24) How would this person's friends describe him or her?

25) How would an enemy describe this person?

26) What is unexpected about the person?

27) HOW IS THIS PERSON LIKE THE PEOPLE

28) How did or do the people you're writing about feel about change in general? What about a particular change?

29) What action(s) might they take as a result of this change?

30) What got or will get better because of the change? What did or will get worse because of it?

31) How might or did the person change/grow/learn? What kinds of events could/would cause this to happen?

32) What would this person change if he/she could? How does he or she try to do so?

33) What does the person hate doing? What circumstances might cause the person to have to do it?

34) What would it be handy for your person to do but he or she can't? Who might he or she have to depend on for help and under what circumstances? OR How might they learn to do it?

35) What does your person love to do? How can you use that?

36) What does the person choose to wear and why? Who doesn't like it and what happens when he/she dresses that way anyway?

37) How does you're the person feel about family? Who does he/she fight with? Who is loving?

38) Is the person a conformist or a rebel? Is that going to change during the course of the book and if so how and as a result of what events?

39) What has the person never told anyone?

40) What rituals, if any change—and how can you use these changes to show the reader the person has changed?

41) Are the rituals and traditions one person wants to follow in conflict with the rituals and traditions someone else wants to follow? How might they change over the course of the book?

42) What were the hopes and dreams and fears of those involved in this event or discovery or time period or using the technique you are describing? (If you are writing a memoir, this is the most important question to ask yourself—ESPECIALLY about anyone you consider a villain of the piece.)(If you are writing self-help, it's useful for readers to know WHY someone in a case history was willing to use your technique to make these changes.)

43) How did (whatever you're writing about) impact their lives?

44) What is the significance to individuals other than those you are specifically writing about? (In other words, how can you go from a narrow focus to a global focus? How can you generalize the specific?)

45) What drove people involved to do what they did?

46) In what ways are these people like the people who will read your book? What do they have in common—readers and people in your book? (This will help create an emotional connection between reader and material.)

47) What were their failures as well as their successes?

48) What else is important to note about the people in your book?

What happens in your book or what points do you want to make?

For each section ask:

1) Where and when does this event or section take place?

2) Why is this event or section important?

3) Who is involved?

4) WHAT CHANGES AS A RESULT OF THIS EVENT OR HOW DOES THIS IMPACT ONE OR MORE PEOPLE YOU WILL INCLUDE IN THE DISCUSSION? (Who changes/grows or could change or grow? How? If it's history or a memoir, how did this inevitably lead to later events?) Another way to look at this is to ask: How did someone's story change as a result of this event or information?

5) Any other details you can think of about the event or section.

6) What do you most want to say about this point or event? Who does it affect? What case studies might you have to back it up? What exercises might reinforce this point?

7) What is EMOTIONALLY important about this event or section?

Deciding on a Structure for your book:

1) Think about nonfiction books you really admire. What worked for you with those books? What didn't?

2) Is there an expected format for the kind of book you want to write? Do you want to follow that format or try something very different? If you try something different, how will you still meet reader expectations?

3) Who are the people impacted by these issues and/or this information? What are their primary concerns? What do they care about?

4) Keeping in mind the people you want to reach, what are the points you want to make?

5) What are some of the stories you would use or facts you would provide to support the points you want to make? Do you want to include charts or graphs or photographs or exercises?

Sensory details:

Note: These may or may not be appropriate in your nonfiction book. I include this just in case it would be useful for you.

Note: You may want to include how the people in your book FEEL/FELT about each of these things. Some may be neutral Most have probably never stopped to think about them but...perhaps one or more has.

1) What is the setting? Rural? Urban? Suburban? Alien/foreign? Be as specific as you can—not by the name of the locale but its characteristics.

2) What kinds of buildings are there? What are they made out of? What kind of comforts do or don't they have?

3) What kinds of stores exist? What are they like? What is the process of shopping like for the people in YOUR book? What stores do which people notice and use? What do people in your book make for themselves instead of buying?

4) What kind of transportation exists? What does it look, sound, and perhaps smell like? What are the good things and what are the challenges with that kind of transportation?

5) What do people eat and drink? How does it taste and smell? Do people use utensils (what kind?) or eat with their hands? What's a luxury? What's common, every day?

6) What occupations and diversions exist? (How do people dress for those things? Where do they do them?)

7) What kind of plumbing and trash disposal exists?

8) What is the weather like?

9) What is the landscape like?

10) How do key characters or people in your book:

Look

Dress

Move

Sound

Smell

11) How do key objects (which may include rooms in a house):

Look

Taste

Feel

Smell

Sound

Details useful to show not tell:

Again, this may or may not be appropriate for the nonfiction book you are writing. If it is, then for each person:

1) List 5 things that scare him or her.

2) List 5 things that make him or her feel safe

3) List 5 physical reactions he or she has when scared

4) List 5 things he or she does when unsure of himself or herself

5) List 5 things he or she does when feeling safe and/or happy

Brainstorming Exercises--for Nonfiction:

1) Introduction: Why are you writing this book?

2) Who is this book for?

3) Why should readers care?

4) What DO your readers care about?

5) What is your conclusion or summary of ideas?

6) What are your key points? (It's okay if you don't yet know how you will lay them out. For now, just figure out what they are.)

7) For each key point, what are the most important comments to make?

8) Are you going to use anecdotes? Case histories? Jot down some notes.

9) Do you want to include any exercises? What would they be?

MEMOIRS

Basic Memoirs—If You Don't Know Where to Begin

Close your eyes and think of the time you want to write about. Try to picture it as vividly as possible—as if you were still there.

1) What are the sounds you remember?

2) What are the sights you remember?

3) What are the smells you remember?

4) What are the foods you remember?

5) What is your physical state? (Were you thin? Plump? Healthy? Sick? Tall? Short?)

6) Where are you?

7) What are the places you remember?

8) How do you feel?

9) What are your hopes and dreams?

10) What are your fears and challenges?

11) Who are your favorite people? Why?

12) What makes you laugh? Cry? Scares you?

13) What are the best things about this time in your life?

14) What are the worst things about this time in your life?

15) Who are the most important—not necessarily your favorite but the most important—people in your life at this time? Why?

16) What are the most important things that are happening? Why are these events so significant to you?

17) What have you never told anyone about this time in your life?

Specific Experience That Matters to You

1) **WHY** does this matter to **YOU**?

2) What is it you want readers to **FEEL**? (Ex: laugh, cry, understand, anger, feel uplifted, etc.)

3) Where did the event(s) take place? Write down everything you can remember about the place **AND HOW IT MADE YOU FEEL**.

4) Who was there and/or involved even if they were not physically present?

5) Did you include yourself?

6) Write down everything you know about each person—including yourself.

7) What were your hopes and fears and dreams during this time?

8) For each person listed in 4), write down their hopes and dreams and fears they had at the time.

9) What happened? Create a time line listing each major event.

10) What was the most significant moment or event? **WHY**? What did you **FEEL**?

11) What did each event mean to you? How did it fit in with your hopes and dreams and fears?

12) What did each event mean to each of the other people present? Again, remember to note how it was tied into each person's hopes and dreams and fears.

13) What was the outcome for each person present or involved? How did they **FEEL**?

14) What was the outcome for **YOU**—both short and long term?

15) What **GOOD** came out of this or what good could you or have you created out of this? (Note: This is the most empowering question you can ask yourself about any difficult or traumatic experience in your life.)

More Memoir Brainstorming Questions

1) What are the events you want to write about?

2) Why are these events important?

3) How did these events impact YOU emotionally?

4) Why do you hope they will be important to readers of your book?

5) What people will be in your memoir and what is important about them?

6) How did each person impact YOU emotionally?

7) For each person, what were their hopes and dreams and fears as these events were occurring?

8) What were YOUR hopes and dreams and fears as these events were occurring?

9) Look again at whoever you perceive as the "villain" of the experience (if there is one). It is especially important to know or try to imagine the hopes and dreams and fears of that person.

10) What did each person do that was memorable and WHY was it memorable?

11) What didn't you know about them at the time of the events that you know now?

12) What do you know about each person very few other people know?

13) What don't you know about them that you should before you write this book?

14) What good came out of the experience and/or what good could you create out of the experience?

PREPARATION FOR BOOK IN A WEEK

Real Life Preparation:

1) Warn your family (or don't warn them if they are saboteurs!).

2) Plan easy meals, make some ahead of time and freeze them or post take-out numbers by the phone.

3) Mow the lawn or do fix-it chores before the week starts.

4) Get the laundry done ahead of time or teach your family to do it.

5) Schedule meetings to take place before or after the writing week.

6) Let co-workers know you need to write during lunch rather than going out with them.

7) Stock up on healthy snacks and music to listen to as you write.

8) Make sure you have pens, paper, or whatever else you may need.

9) Ask for support.

Mental/Emotional Preparation:

1) Decide why you are doing Book In A Week. (Note: I'm assuming you're writing the first draft of your book and want to try this as a method of doing so. Sometimes people have other reasons as well.) Examples:

   a) You have a deadline to meet.

   b) You want to try something new, have no idea how it will work out, and don't want to invest a lot of time to find out.

   c) You feel burned out and need to have fun again with your writing.

   d) You are writing books in a series.

   e) You are writing difficult material and it helps to know that you will only be immersed in it for a week.

   f) You want to discover what you can do and who you are as a writer.

   g) You just want to write faster and better.

   h) You're trying to decide between two projects and not sure which one will work.

2) Remind yourself that you will keep writing—no matter what. Tell yourself that it's only one week and if it doesn't work, if you turn out trash, so what? It's only one week of your life. Picture shoving that inner critic into the closet and padlocking the door! Or keep a mental two by four or baseball bat handy.

Writing Preparation:

1) Get a sense of what you want to write, your characters, setting, and plot—an outline if that works for you and/or use index cards to plan out your story.

2) Use the exercises in this workbook to get a sense of some of the things you need to know beforehand.

3) For nonfiction, study the sort of book you want to write. What expectations will readers/editors have? What format do you like/not like? Will you need to include anecdotes, charts, and photos?

4) Get a folder for all your notes, research notes, character sketches, outlines, etc. Keep it handy while writing.

If you know you need to do research, try to do it before the week begins, otherwise keep any research books you will need right next to where you work to minimize the time needed to check them.

5) Get a notebook and/or voice recorder or figure out how to make notes with an app on your smart phone so that whenever you need to leave your writing area—to run errands, etc.—you can take it along and either work on a scene or make notes for what you will write when you get back to the computer.

6) Have a notebook in which you can jot down real life things you remember you will need to do when you take a break.

BOOK IN A WEEK

Actual Writing Week

1) Write. Keep writing. Do not go back and reread what you've written—this alone can speed up your writing process immensely.

2) If something comes up, take care of it then go back to writing. (I've had to deal with doctor's appointments, school meetings and day-to-day crises during BIAW. You go back to where you were and keep writing.)

3) Keep that notebook handy to immediately jot down day to day life things you think of that will need to be taken care of WHEN YOU TAKE A BREAK. That way your brain won't be focused on those things while you are trying to write.

4) If you have an off morning or day, don't beat yourself up—just get back to writing and keep going.

5) If you only have 5 minutes at a time, sit down and write for 5 minutes! (I've had days like that and ended up with 27 pages!)

6) Ignore any and all attempts to self-censor or edit. Put in asterisks or whatever symbol you like for things you will need to research or decide on later—including names of characters. Just write! (Note: It often helps to put notes to yourself in a different colored font or to highlight that text so you can spot it quickly when you go back through later.)

7) Carry a notebook or voice recorder or index cards everywhere (unless you can make notes on your smart phone). Every spare minute you have, jot down ideas for the project you are working on or even write scenes. (Note: Do NOT transcribe these scenes into the computer until AFTER Book In A Week is over. Instead, make a note on the computer that you have a scene to insert and KEEP GOING—otherwise the temptation to revise as you transcribe is likely to be too great.) If nothing else, you are telling your subconscious to stay focused on the book.

8) If you have trouble typing for long periods of time, you may want to look into a voice recognition (to text) program. Probably not ideal to start using it during this week, but keep it in mind for the future.

9) If you make changes, KEEP GOING! You will fix earlier writing AFTER the writing week is over and the first draft is done. If you go back and change things, you may lose something important.

10) If you think of something new to insert in an earlier part of the book, you have two choices. If you have iron will power and can just go back and write the new material WITHOUT rewriting the surrounding material, do so. If not, go back and insert notes into that file on the computer. (Highlight these notes so you don't miss them when you revise!) Or simply write down a note to yourself and put it in that folder you keep handy while you

work. If you don't know a character's name, use a place marker such as Xx or Yy. (Avoid things like Tt or Ss since those combinations often occur in words and you'll have a mess when you do search and replace later.)

11) Eat nutritious foods, drink plenty of water. Cut up fruit or veggies or cheese or a bowl of prepared salad in the refrigerator can be a lifesaver when you are in the middle of BIAW.

12) Make sure you get up and stretch and move around at least once an hour. Just the act of moving can shake things up and get you past a sticking point.

13) If you get ideas for another project, take 5 minutes and jot them down on index cards—THEN GO BACK TO WRITING!

14) Make notes for things you will need to research so that after the writing week is over, you can do the research and fill in the information on the index cards and have it handy.

15) Jot down things you realize about your characters on their index cards. Just key words. Don't take a lot of time on this but if you have, say a valet, and you name him Cranford, you will be profoundly glad you noted it on his index card if 6 chapters later you need to know if a) you've already used the name Cranford or b) the valet reappears and you can't remember his name!

16) Let others know how you are doing. Have at least one person to whom you tell your daily total of pages written—it will keep you writing even when you don't feel like doing so. This is NOT a competition but an incentive to keep writing. Keep writing! (Are you starting to notice a theme?)

Each Day As You Begin to Write

1) As you sit down to write, close your eyes for a moment and remember what it was like to play make believe as a child. Remember a time when the writing just flowed and felt wonderful.

2) Picture the words flowing. Imagine finishing the manuscript and putting it in the mail. Imagine the call from an editor asking to buy the book.

3) Picture yourself accepting an award for your book. Picture signing copies for adoring fans.

If You Get Stuck

1) Jump to the next scene and keep going. Go back and fill in later.

2) Start throwing in anything you can think of! You can always take it out later but you may be surprised how well it works.

3) Change HOW you are writing. ((Ex: Long hand vs. computer vs. tablet vs. voice recorder).)

4) Change WHERE you write. Just moving into another room or outside can sometimes help. If your family isn't letting you work, go to the library or a coffee shop to write.

5) Change WHEN you write. Some people write better in the morning, others at night and you may want to experiment this week to discover what works best for YOU.

6) If you seem to be getting nowhere, try writing in short blocks—15 minutes at a time, followed by 5 minute breaks and then writing again.

7) Get up and move around for a couple of minutes. In fact, if you are writing steadily, you should get up and move around for at least 5 minutes every hour anyway.

At The End Of Each Day

1) BACK UP YOUR WORK

2) Let someone SUPPORTIVE know how it went.

3) Think about what you wrote. How it ties together. Where you might go with it tomorrow. MAKE NOTES FOR YOURSELF on what you need to write the next day. (You are NOT going to reread your work of the day before! It's just one week—try it as an experiment. Start from your notes of the night before and you'll be amazed at how well that can work.)

4) Take a few minutes—after you make your notes for the next day—to unwind.

5) Every day, at the end of your writing day, CELEBRATE being a writer and having the guts/determination to sit down and write. This is as important as any other step in the process!

6) Each day take a moment to imagine your book on the best seller list.

7) Before you go to sleep ask your subconscious to work on any unresolved issues in your book--especially those you need for the next day.

EVALUATING THE BOOK IN A WEEK EXPERIENCE

Practical Matters

1) Where was the best place for you to write? Why?

2) Where was it hard to write? Why?

3) When was the best time for you to write? Why?

4) When was the worst time for you to write? Why?

5) What was the best method for you—longhand, computer, tape recorder, etc?

6) What method didn't work for you?

7) Who was helpful and who acted as a saboteur?

8) Where in your day could you fit more time to write or to make notes for your writing?

9) What was the best thing to do when you got stuck?

10) What DIDN'T work when you got stuck?

How You Write

1) Are you a fast or slow writer?

2) Did you write a longer first draft than you need or a shorter one?

3) What made you most want to stop?

4) What made you most want to keep writing?

5) What made it the most fun? How can you incorporate more of that into your everyday writing life?

6) Did you find you wrote better when you used long blocks of time or short blocks of time?

7) What--if any--visualizations worked best for you?

Who You Are As A Writer--Fiction?

1) Which came naturally--character or plot?

2) Did you write lots of description or did you write more action?

3) What about your characters do you most love and/or hate?

Who You Are As A Writer--Nonfiction?

1) Did you include exercises? Why or why not?

2) What ways did you naturally use to make your points? Case histories? Facts? Stories?

3) Did your writing fall into a natural pattern dividing up the material?

4) What resonates with you in terms of the structure you used?

5) What style did you find yourself using? Is it most natural to you or did you choose it because of what you were writing about? Is it something you'll want to use again?

Who You Are As A Writer--Both Fiction and Nonfiction?

1) What themes or emotions or people/characters or situations most resonated with you?

2) What makes you most want to smile about your work?

3) What do you see as your natural strengths?

4) What do you see as your natural weaknesses?

5) What did you love about what you wrote?

6) What still needed work?

7) If you tried something new, did you like it?

8) If you did not like what you tried, why not? What else might you like to try?

9) If you tried something new, what did you discover you didn't/don't yet know about writing this kind of project?

Author's Note

I hope you found these exercises useful. If you are curious about my other books, you can find more information here: http://www.aprilkihlstrom.com.

If you would like to take my online Book in a Week--or any other online writing class, you can sign up here to be notified when I will be teaching an online class: http://groups.yahoo.com/group/aprilkihlstromwritingclasses2/join.

Note: If you send me proof of purchase for either this workbook or my Book in a Week book when you sign up for my Book in a Week class, you will get a 10% discount on the price of the class.

If you found this workbook useful, I hope you will post a review. Thank you!

PICTURES

NOTES

CHARACTER LIST

Made in the USA
San Bernardino, CA
19 March 2014